What Do... Construction Workers Do?

Emma Juhasz

Mighty Shepherd Publishing

Wates

Illustrations by Amanda Lillywhite

Thank You!

Special thanks to Kate Ives & Michelle McSorley
at Wates for your enthusiasm and support.

Also, the following people for giving up their time
to help with research and production of the book.

Lucy Abbott – Wates
Amelia Breadman – JTP Architects
Katherine Doha – Wates
Jennie Ellis – Wates
Stuart Hamilton – Wates
Matthew Harvey – Avison Young
Marina Lazaar – Clarkebond
Kiara Long – SAY Property Consulting LLP
Thomas Lule – Wates
David Saunders – Wates
Sam Spittles – CBRE Group

Amanda Lillywhite for her brilliant drawings.

Published in the United Kingdom by:
Emma Juhasz
www.emmajuhasz.com

A CIP record of this book is available at the British Library.

First printed September 2020.

ISBN Number 978-1-9996494-1-8

Contents

About Wates

Wates   Wates is one of biggest construction
         companies in the UK and has been
owned by one family for over 120 years. The
company builds and sells new homes, constructs
public buildings, like schools, offices and leisure
centres. It also maintains 500,000 homes across
the country every year.

Nearly 4,000 people work for Wates in jobs
that are included in this book.

To find out more about Wates you can visit:
www.wates.co.uk

About Emma

Emma has worked
closely with Wates,
to create this fun and
informative insight into
the construction industry.

As a children's non-fiction
author, Emma wants to
create books that help
children learn about jobs
and begin to think about their own future, from
an early age. This was first seen in her popular
and well-reviewed debut, What Do Vets Do?,
published by Mighty Shepherd Publishing.

Discover more about Emma, her news and
reviews at: www.emmajuhasz.com

What is
Construction?

What is Construction?
▶ building the future

Construction means to build something.

What do you build?

Anything, such as flats, houses, shops, cinemas, hospitals, schools, roads and sports centres.

Where do you build?

Places that need knocking down and rebuilding, as they are very old; or on land that is not built on yet.

Who works in construction?

So many people, all doing very different things. Depending on how big the project is, there could be 50, 100s or 1000s of people involved.

How long does it take to construct something?

Smaller projects can take about 3 or 4 months, bigger ones can take years. There is also a lot of work that happens before building work can start. Drawings need to be done, which show what it will look like outside and in, the council* needs to give permission to build the project and then you need to find all the right people to build it. It can take a long time!

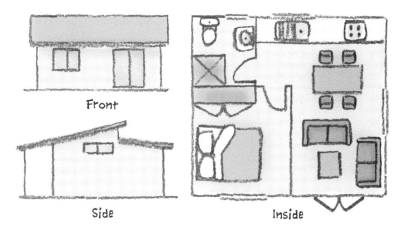

Front

Side

Inside

*See Construction Words on page 48.

Tools of the Trade
▶ designing the construction

Some items used to design a construction project may look like things you find in your pencil case, or at school. This could include pencils, drawing pens, rulers, tracing paper, glue, measuring tape, modelling clay, cutting boards and knives (only used by your teacher!).

Other items you may not see at school:

Construction calculator
Different to normal calculators, they solve construction maths problems: such as measurements or amount of material needed.

Drawing table
for doing large drawings.

Electronic Distance Measurer (EDM).
This is used to measure long distances, instead of using a measuring tape or ruler.

3D* printer
a machine that will make a model of the construction.

Tools of the Trade

▶ building the construction

There are many tools and pieces of equipment used on a construction site* – big and small. Here are some of the main ones:

Big Machines

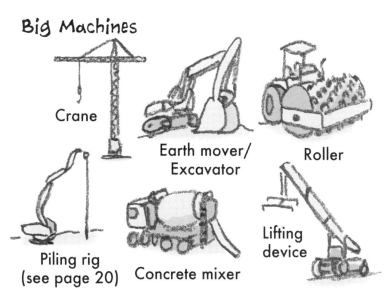

Crane

Earth mover/ Excavator

Roller

Piling rig (see page 20)

Concrete mixer

Lifting device

A Worker's Toolkit

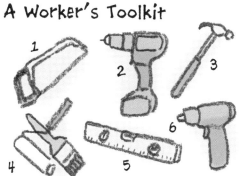

1 Saw
2 Power drill
3 Hammer
4 Paintbrush
5 Spirit level – makes sure everything is straight
6 Electric screwdriver

*See Construction Words on page 48.

9

Activity

▶ super structures

Create your own amazing constructions. How many can you put together? How tall and how wide can you go without it falling over?

What do you need?

✳ Mini marshmallows or sweets, like jelly babies

✳ Toothpicks

Start by building a square, rectangle or triangle.

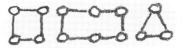

Add more layers to create a cube, cuboid or pyramid.

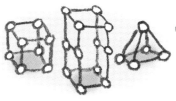

Then keep going!

Top Tip! Make sure the bottom part of your construction has a wide base to support the building as it gets bigger.

Construction
in Action

Meet the Team
▶ jobs in construction

Oliver
Town Planner
In charge of what, where and how cities/buildings are developed.
See pages 16 + 17 to find out more.

Ella
Architect
Designs buildings.
See pages 18 + 19 to find out more.

Mo
Civil Engineer
Works out and solves construction problems, before work starts.
See page 20 to find out more.

Lily
Structural Engineer
Makes buildings
stand up and stay up.
See page 21 to find
out more.

Arthur
Project Manager
In charge of the
building site.
See pages 22 + 23
to find out more.

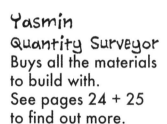

Yasmin
Quantity Surveyor
Buys all the materials
to build with.
See pages 24 + 25
to find out more.

Theo
BIM Manager
Makes 3D plans of
the whole building.
See pages 26 + 27
to find out more.

Meet the Team
▶ jobs in construction

Olivia
Sales Manager
Sells the building.
See page 30 to
find out more.

Ali
Estate Manager
Looks after the
building once
it is built.
See page 31
to find out more.

Site Workers
There are so many
site worker jobs, too
many to show them all,
but come and meet
some of the main ones,
such as Sophie the
crane operator.

See pages 28 + 29 to find out more.

Construction Clothes

▶ stay safe on site

Construction sites are busy places with lots of people doing many different jobs using big machines and different tools; as well as people working at great heights. Safety is very important, which is why you need to wear special safety clothes.

Everyone has to wear a hard hat on site, to protect their head from bumps or from objects if they fall.

Safety Goggles are worn all the time, to protect the eyes.

Everyone needs to be seen, so they wear a high-vis jacket or vest (brightly coloured top, which reflects the light).

A tough pair of gloves must be worn to protect hands from sharp objects, cuts and burns.

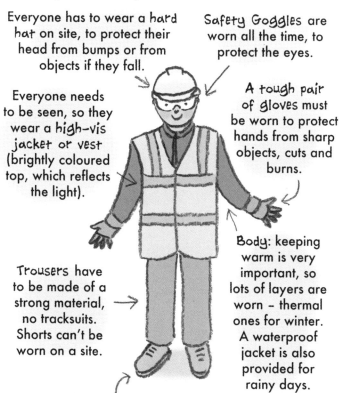

Body: keeping warm is very important, so lots of layers are worn – thermal ones for winter. A waterproof jacket is also provided for rainy days.

Trousers have to be made of a strong material, no tracksuits. Shorts can't be worn on a site.

Big boots with metal on the toes (in case something drops on them).

15

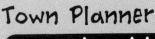

Town Planner

▶ creating cities

Oliver is showing a developer* that badgers are living in a field that she wants to build on. Oliver knows that all animals must be protected. The developer will need to show Oliver how her new building will not harm where the badgers live. She will also need to explain how she will protect them from the building work.

Oliver is telling councillors* about plans to knock down some old flats and construct new houses. He also wants to add more trees, playgrounds and cycle lanes, in the area. The councillors will say 'yes' or 'no' to whether this can be built.

What do they do?

Town Planners help work out what, where, how and why new buildings, shops, parks and even whole cities are built. They make sure all new constructions help people and nature.

*See Construction Words on page 48.

Architect

Ella is making a wooden 3D model of her new design for a block of flats. This shows Ella what the flats will look like when they are built, it also helps her see if there are any problems with the design.

What do they do?
An architect will design what a building will look like. The building needs to look good, as well as be safe and comfortable to live in.

Construction in Action

Ella is with a Project Manager on a site for a block of flats. She is checking everything is being built as it was drawn on her plans. They are looking at some windows and are making sure that they have been put in the right place.

Civil Engineer
▶ problems solved

Mo is at a new site, which is by the sea. He is using a special machine to collect samples from the different layers of soil, sand, clay and rock that are under the ground.

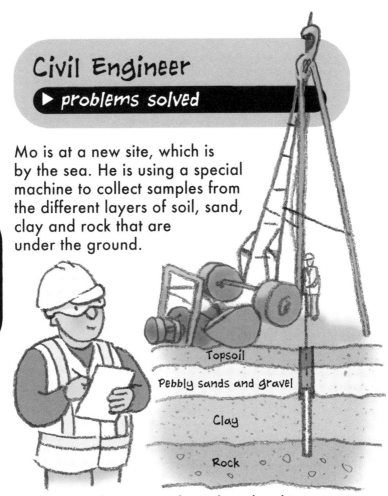

Topsoil

Pebbly sands and gravel

Clay

Rock

From these, he can work out how hard it would be to dig in the area and what type of foundations* the new building will need, so it does not fall over or sink.

What do they do?
Civil engineers work out and solve problems about where and how something is to be built.

*See Construction Words on page 48.

Structural Engineer
▶ balancing buildings

Lily is with some school children, showing them how to design a balcony. She has asked the children to see how long they can hold out their arm completely straight, now Lily is about to add a weight, a school bag. How long before the children bend/drop their arm?

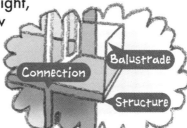

Connection

Balustrade

Structure

A building has to hold the weight of a balcony forever, so Lily needs to make sure it is not too heavy, so the balcony doesn't bend or break off.

What do they do?
Structural engineers look at the architect's plan and then work out how to make a building stand up and stay up.

21

Project Manager
▶ managing sites

A piling rig has been delivered to Arthur's site. This is a huge machine which pushes large columns into the ground. These columns form the bottom part of a building.

Arthur knows someone could get hurt with such a large machine on the site, so he is talking to his workers about safety, including using the new path that has been marked out with barriers around the rig.

The building is nearly finished! Arthur has to check the building work all the time now, so everything is done well. He is making sure that a bathroom pod (the bathroom is sent to the site in a box, it is built in a factory and delivered ready to use) is placed in the right room and safely, which can be a difficult task when you are three floors up!

What do they do?
Project Managers are in charge of everyone and everything on a building site. They make sure everyone is safe, that the construction is built as it is shown on the plans and will be finished by a certain day.

Quantity Surveyor

▶ supplying buildings

Yasmin needs to be good at maths! She is working out from a 3D digital model* of a block of flats, how many bricks are needed to build the whole building. Yasmin has to get the bricks from a country called Holland and it takes nearly 4 months for them to arrive, so she needs to try to get the right amount at the start. Not always easy!

980,900?

1,100,000?

1,000,500?

Yasmin needs to be good at talking to and working with many different people. She is with the bricklayer, site manager and developer. They have run out of bricks and cannot finish the walls. Yasmin wants to use a different type of brick which she has on site, but the developer is not happy as they do not look like the other ones. Everyone agrees to stop work, while Yasmin orders some new bricks.

What do they do?
Quantity Surveyors are in charge of buying all the materials for a construction project, such as doors, windows and bricks. They also employ* people and pay for everything on site.

*See Construction Words on page 48.

BIM Manager
▶ digital constructions

Theo has put together an architect's and engineer's designs for a new building, on his BIM computer. It shows that their measurements are different, as walls and pipes are at different heights. They will need to redo their designs.

Theo is at a school showing a headteacher some 3D plans, on a VR headset*, for a new classroom at her school. She can see from this that the classroom needs to be bigger and have more windows. Theo will put this information on the BIM model, so the design is changed and made better.

What do they do?
BIM (Building Information Modelling) Manager creates 3D digital models, which show all the designs and information, from the beginning until the end, about a construction project. It makes it easier to design, build and look after a building.

*See Construction Words on page 48.

Site Workers
▶ building sites

There are so many different jobs you can do, here are some of them:

Bricklayer
Charlie will put together a building's walls, often he uses bricks which are stuck together with mortar*.

Crane Operator
Sophie works a crane, which lifts, moves and places heavy loads around the site.

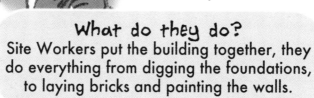

Carpenter
Josh cuts, makes and puts in wooden or plastic parts of the building, such as doorframes, floors and kitchen cupboards.

What do they do?
Site Workers put the building together, they do everything from digging the foundations, to laying bricks and painting the walls.

Note: These workers would always wear the safety clothes (see page 15) when working on a site.

Painter

Mia paints walls, floors, windows of buildings and can even paint large structures like bridges.

Electrician

Omar looks after all the electricity*, he puts in electrical wires and plug sockets, which make the heating and lights work.

Construction in Action

Roofer

Lulu needs good balance, as she hammers in the wood and tiles on the roof.

Plumber

Moses puts in all the pipes that bring water into a building, such as for drinking, showers and toilets.

Excavator (Digger)

Matthew uses the digger to dig up and move lots of soil, to make foundations or holes on the construction site.

*See Construction Words on page 48.

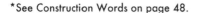

Sales Manager
▶ **selling buildings**

Construction in Action

Olivia is in a special building called a marketing suite. It is found next to a building site and it shows people who want to buy a flat or house, what everything will look like when it is finished. Olivia is showing people the kitchen area.

What do they do?
Before buildings are built, people in Sales will help work out what it could look like and how much it could cost. Then they help sell it, before and after it's built.

Estate Manager
▶ managing buildings

Ali is in the basement of a block of flats. The machine which keeps everyone warm in their flats has broken. Ali and an engineer are trying to work out how to mend it.

What do they do?
The Estate Manager looks after a building once it has been built, keeping it clean and safe. They care for everyone who lives and works in the building, as well as the building itself; such as the gardens, heating and electricity.

31

Activity

▶ construct a story

See how many of the pictures you can use, to create your own story. You can do it on your own or with a friend.

Brilliant
Builds

Where in the World?

▶ great constructions

Space Needle Tower, Seattle, USA

Harpa Concert Hall, Reykjavik, Iceland

Confederation Bridge, over Abegweit Passage, Canada

One World Trade Center (Freedom Tower) New York, USA

The White House, Washington DC, USA

Las Lajas Sanctuary, Nariño, Colombia

Pyramid of the Sun, Teotihuacan, Mexico

Amazing constructions have been and are still being built all the time. Let's explore the world and discover where some of them are. Look them up on a computer with your Mum, Dad or teacher. Which building do you like best? Why?

Machu Picchu, Andes Mountains, Peru

St Paul's Cathedral, London

Mont-St-Michel, Normandy, France

Himeji Castle, Himeji, Japan

Dancing House, Prague, Czechoslovakia

Forbidden City, Beijing, China

Potala Palace, Lhasa, Tibet

Dome of the Rock, Jerusalem, Israel

Petronas Towers, Kuala Lumpur, Malaysia

Taj Mahal, Agra, India

Guggenheim Museum, Bilbao, Spain

Sydney Opera House, Australia

Brilliant Builds

Building Through Time

▶ changes in construction

What? Pyramids
Where? Egypt
When? 2589–2504 BC (85 years to build)
Why? To protect the bodies of the dead pharaohs (kings).
How big? There are 80 pyramids, the largest is the Great Pyramid of Giza: 456 feet high.
Did you know? The entrances to all the pyramids face to the north.

What? Great Wall of China
Where? Northern China
When? 770 BC–1878 (2,648 years to build)
Why? To protect China from enemy attacks.
How long was it? 13,700 miles long – lots of it has fallen down now.
Did you know? It's not one long wall, but lots of walls joined together.

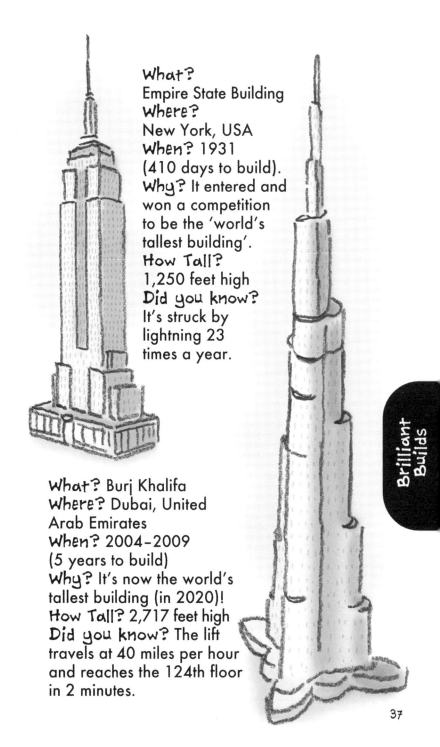

What?
Empire State Building
Where?
New York, USA
When? 1931
(410 days to build).
Why? It entered and
won a competition
to be the 'world's
tallest building'.
How Tall?
1,250 feet high
Did you know?
It's struck by
lightning 23
times a year.

What? Burj Khalifa
Where? Dubai, United
Arab Emirates
When? 2004–2009
(5 years to build)
Why? It's now the world's
tallest building (in 2020)!
How Tall? 2,717 feet high
Did you know? The lift
travels at 40 miles per hour
and reaches the 124th floor
in 2 minutes.

Brilliant
Builds

Deep Underground

▶ buried treasure

While construction is about creating something new, often it first reveals something amazing and old. Archaeologists*, scientists and even bomb disposal experts* help out on construction sites when the digging of foundations starts, as extraordinary things are found deep underground (here are just some of them).

WW2 Bomb

Unexploded (didn't blow up) bomb from World War 2 (1939-1945).

Ice Skates

900 years ago, people used bones attached to their shoes for ice skates.

Woolly Mammoth Jawbone

Hairy elephants (no longer alive) with huge tusks lived in Great Britain over 100,000 years ago.

CAUTION!
ARCHAEOLOGISTS
AT WORK

Skulls/Bones

Skeletons are often found, 3,300 were at one site, all dating from 1665.

Roman Villa Pots

Romans (people from Italy) lived in England & Wales about 1,500 years ago. They left many things including houses, forts, coins and pots.

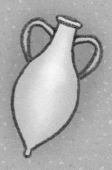

*See Construction Words on page 48.

Activity

▶ dig for words

Can you find the construction words below, they are hidden in these letters? *Remember they can be written down, up, forwards, backwards and sideways!*

Words to find:

ARCHITECT	SITE
DIGGER	MODEL
PLANNER	BIM
CRANE	BRICK
ENGINEER	SURVEYOR

M	A	C	J	R	L	V	E	A	U	E	N	V	D	G
K	Y	Y	O	C	N	U	E	U	H	H	R	Y	S	Y
L	F	H	X	V	P	C	S	V	S	K	S	A	H	Z
Q	K	H	M	I	B	G	E	K	S	K	A	V	E	Y
M	M	C	K	P	L	A	N	N	E	R	C	C	N	J
H	O	K	D	A	D	S	R	Y	F	J	O	I	A	Z
J	D	X	I	X	K	Y	V	C	E	F	P	P	R	E
D	E	E	R	E	P	F	K	X	H	I	J	M	C	B
X	L	H	E	F	D	H	N	G	M	I	J	T	M	E
O	T	D	Q	I	L	G	N	P	X	Y	T	R	W	A
R	L	R	G	G	G	B	B	L	M	L	K	E	Q	O
U	W	G	W	E	S	U	R	V	E	Y	O	R	C	I
R	E	M	J	G	W	G	W	V	X	I	Q	G	I	T
R	A	R	S	B	C	E	T	I	S	Y	D	I	W	R
H	A	D	O	D	R	E	E	N	I	G	N	E	H	F

Answers on page 48.

Brilliant Builds

40

Building your Future

Building your Future
▶ you can work in construction

There are so many different and exciting things you can do in construction. Let's get you on the right track, so you can work in construction too!

Start

You can study more for most jobs in construction, if you want to. However! You have to go to university to become an architect, engineer or town planner. Once you have worked for a while, you can even change your construction job: e.g. architects become BIM managers, carpenters become project managers etc.

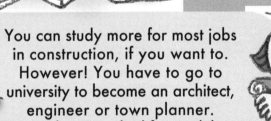

Top tips for working in construction!

✱ Be happy to work with many people.

✱ Be ready to work out how to make people's homes and lives better.

✱ Be excited – every day is so different!

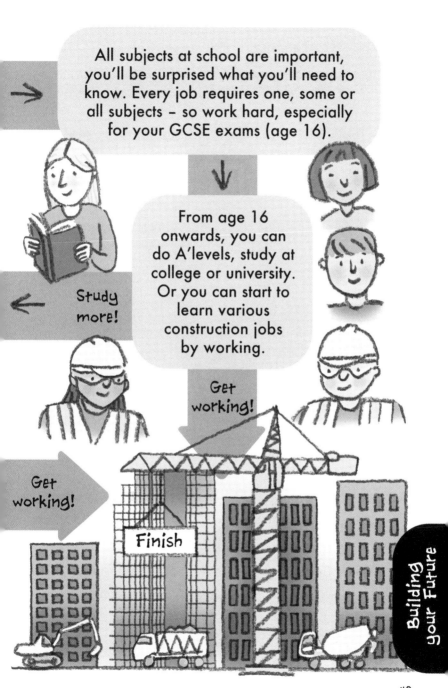

All subjects at school are important, you'll be surprised what you'll need to know. Every job requires one, some or all subjects – so work hard, especially for your GCSE exams (age 16).

Study more!

From age 16 onwards, you can do A'levels, study at college or university. Or you can start to learn various construction jobs by working.

Get working!

Get working!

Finish

Building your Future

Building your Future

▶ you can build it!

Get ready to work in construction by playing these brilliant games!

Building with Lego and blocks are great for learning how construction works.

✳ Build them up, knock them down, time how quickly they fall down.

✳ Follow a Lego building booklet to create something.

Construct a family outing and visit some of these places. Check websites for locations.
Diggerland www.diggerland.com
Science Museum www.sciencecentres.org.uk
The Building Centre www.buildingcentre.co.uk
Imagine That! www.imaginethat.org.uk

Use computer games, such as Minecraft and Block Craft, to design your own houses and cities.

Work out how to put it together.

Do a picture puzzle, balance shapes together or make a marble run out of building blocks like Lego.

Activity

▶ draw your own

How to draw buildings.

1  Draw a straight line.

2 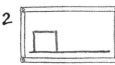 Draw a rectangle shape on the line.

3 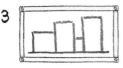 Draw another and another – make them bigger or smaller, fatter or thinner.

4 Draw windows and doors on your buildings. You could also add a footpath, road, sky, trees, whatever you like. Then colour it all in.

Draw your building here!

Building your Future

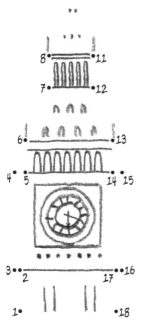

Join the dots to find London's famous clock tower.

Did you know that Big Ben is not the name of the clock tower? Can you find out what IS called Big Ben?

Draw your face on this construction worker and colour them in.

What construction job would you like to do?

....

UNDER CONSTRUCTION

Construction Words

Page 7/17 **Council/councillors** A group of people who are elected by the public, to regularly meet up and make decisions about what happens in a city, town, or county.

Page 8 **3D** Everything we see and walk around is in 3D. We do not see in flat images, like pictures in a book (2D). A 3D printer will build a model of a building or room, as we would see it.

Page 9 **Site** An area of ground on which a town or building is constructed.

Page 16 **Developer** A person who decides what they want built and gives the money to construct it.

Page 20 **Foundations** Generally underground, this is the lowest part of a building and the area that takes most of its weight.

Page 24 **3D Digital models** 3D digital models are on a computer, they are images of a building or parts of a building, which look real and are not like a drawing in a book.

Page 25 **Employ** To give someone a job.

Page 27 **VR (Virtual Reality) Headset** The headset is put in front of your eyes, like glasses and shows a computer image. This image can be of anything, but the image looks real (3D), so you think you are there and can walk around it.

Page 28 **Mortar** Made of cement, sand and lime, it is soft and gooey, like putty and it helps stick bricks together. It goes hard when it dries.

Page 29 **Electricity** Like lightning, electricity is a type of energy that flows from one place to another. You can't see it, but it is everywhere. It is put in buildings, so when we turn it on, everything from your television to your lights go on.

Page 38 **Archaeologist** A person who learns and teaches us about people from the past by looking for old things, like pots and bones, which have been found buried in the ground.

Page 38 **Bomb Disposal Experts** People who deal with bombs which have not exploded. They can take out the bomb's fuse or blow it up in a controlled explosion.